TOUCHED BY GOD

WOMEN'S STORIES OF
SPIRITUAL TRANSFORMATION

DOCUMENTED BY

JACQUELINE BERG

Touched by God
Women's Stories of Spiritual Transformation

Jacqueline Berg

First Edition 2006

ISBN No: 1-886872-29-5

Published by Brahma Kumaris Information Services Ltd., in
association with Brahma Kumaris World Spiritual University
(UK) Registered Charity No. 269971.
Global Co-operation House, 65 Pound Lane, London NW10
2HH, UK

Designed by BookDesign™, London
Printed by Power Digital Printing Co Ltd. Hong Kong

www.bkpublications.com
email: enquiries@bkpublications.com

www.bkwsu.org

TOUCHED BY GOD

WOMEN'S STORIES OF
SPIRITUAL TRANSFORMATION

DOCUMENTED BY

JACQUELINE BERG

BK PUBLICATIONS
an imprint of
BRAHMA KUMARIS INFORMATION SERVICES LTD.

PREFACE

THE STORIES IN this book are told by women but they contain a message of hope for all. They describe a range of experiences that shed light on universal predicaments.

What happens when an overactive, restless mind puts a lock on feelings? If that same mind is taught to stop thinking for a while, what does the heart reveal?

How many people are "running on empty" in today's hard-driving world? Why do we shut ourselves off from the good wishes of others? Is there a switch in thinking that will enable us to be easy and giving again, more effective participants in the game of life?

With honesty, clarity and conviction, the contributors to this remarkable book, each in a completely individual way, reveal profound solutions to age-old problems. These personal accounts of transformation offer practical proof of the power of spiritual understanding and renewal.

INTRODUCTION

WHO ARE THESE women who have been touched by God? Are they traditional nuns or modern, spiritual women? Most of them come from a religious background; some were brought up as Christian, some Hindu, Buddhist or Jew. For some of them, their spiritual journey started with a visionary experience. For others, it began with a dream or with whispered words of God. These unknown, remarkable women live across the five continents of the world. They are fully present and active in our modern society. Single or married, with or without a family, in professional life or not, they live with purity and peace. Their deepest commitment is to God to whom they have made the sacred promise to serve the world through their spirituality.

The common thread that binds them is their faith in one God. They are all studying and practising raja yoga meditation with the Brahma Kumaris World Spiritual University, an international spiritual organisation led by women. Brahma Kumaris means daughters of Brahma.

Brahma, the founder of the spiritual university, was an inspiring example who transformed his entire life to become a messenger of peace for the world. A man ahead of his time, Brahma put young women at the forefront of the task of restoring a state of balance and justice in society. These women are still at the head of the university and each one is now known as 'Dadi' (elder sister).

Brahma felt that women were the ideal teachers for people who embark on a spiritual journey. Their qualities of tolerance, wisdom, patience and compassion support others across the stormy seas of sorrow and confusion. Drawing on God's love and power, the Dadis are dedicated to holding a spiritual vision of the human family, a vision that invokes a peaceful life filled with tranquillity, love and happiness.

The spiritual awakening of many of the women in this book has been the result of an intense search for love and truth. Their yearning derived from a deep inner desire to bring spirituality and divinity back into life and to do something significant for the world. Their stories are touching and real; an inspiration for anyone who wishes to make a difference in his or her own life. To make our world a better place to live, these women highlight the need to have a clear look at our inner world of thoughts and feelings, attitudes and awareness.

These are courageous people. They are all consciously transforming their thoughts and feelings, with the power of inner truth. This restores self-respect, vital for harmonious relationships.

Contents

SPIRITUALITY

For most people, spirituality is no longer an alien word. Many now integrate spirituality into their daily life in one way or another. For them, it has become a necessity to take time for the inner self, so that they have the strength to apply spiritual values in their work and relationships.

It's not easy to remain spiritually aware all the time. The habit of being superficial is strong. Breaking through the barriers of spiritual ignorance requires great determination and inner strength. However, when we accept and use support from God, the task will be accomplished easily. This is a special time with special blessings, a time in which the impossible becomes possible.

THE STORIES

Many of these stories were told during conversations in Madhuban, the headquarters of the Brahma Kumaris in Mount Abu, Rajasthan, India. Between all the meetings, programmes and meditations, we found time to sit and talk on the balcony of Sukhdham, a beautiful guesthouse.

It was a special and deep experience to listen to these women talking sincerely about how their lives has been touched by God.

Jacqueline Berg

HAPPINESS

"My ego prevented me from having spiritual experiences. Through my spiritual practice, I slowly learned to open myself to the heart. When the heart and the head work well together, you become happy. You don't have to do anything to be happy. You just are. You think less and you love God."

Sharonah
Educator
Israel/USA

I ALWAYS HAD the feeling that I was supposed to do something special with my life, something that would benefit many, not just myself. I had a lot of ideals and I was committed to living them out in full, even though it wasn't always easy to accommodate such feelings.

In my early adult life, I was successful in all the ways that people usually think of as success. I had a great apartment in the centre of Paris, a great job, great hobbies and satisfying relationships. However, I was discovering that I could never just sit idly on my beautiful couch in my beautiful living room and simply enjoy the life I had created. This was the first indication that I was actually not on the right track. Whatever joy I had in my life came from the dozens of activities that I kept myself busy with. It seemed that I could not be happy, unless I was on the move, active in a variety of ways. I resented this, feeling that it shouldn't have to be such hard work to find a little happiness. Yet every time I tried to relax and *do* nothing, I became depressed and those depressions were certainly telling me that something was wrong, that I was not being true to some more significant purpose.

I even went back to my own religion, Judaism, although it had never really attracted me. I always found it too rigid, too void of feelings, though I could not have explained in these words then. This attempt failed for the same reason: I could find no sense of fulfilment. I then turned to a variety of other spiritual paths, only to discover - usually in the first encounter - that there was nothing for me there either.

When I came across the Brahma Kumaris, I was instantly drawn intellectually. However, that intellectual enthusiasm also carried with it an ego the size of Chicago, Illinois. Eventually I came to understand that it was this ego, feeding off an overworked intellect, that prevented me from being able to open myself to the life-enriching experiences of my inner world. It was ego that was blocking my discovery of true happiness in life.

I gradually began to realise that much of my life had been spent thinking about what life was all about, instead of simply enjoying it. I was spending a lot of time analysing life to understand how everything had gone so wrong. I didn't know then what I know now – that the only way to really be of help to the larger whole is to be the best piece of it that I can be. The key word here is *be*, versus *understand*. It is said that we need to *be* the changes we want to see in others and in the world. Not just *understand* them. Perhaps I grasped this intellectually then. However, I still had no real tools to make it work in daily life.

Finally, I came to the conclusion that I was tired of needing to understand everything. I realised that some of the people I admired most in my life didn't really know how to articulate their values and ideals. Instead, their lives were quite simply a demonstration of those values and ideals. I respected that. I couldn't help noting how I, on the other hand, could talk endlessly about such things, without ever *being* any of them very much at all. Not that I wasn't a good person. I was. But so much of my goodness felt contrived. I was getting tired of 'acting' good. It felt like I was moving further and further away from my ideals for myself. It felt as though I was running on empty.

After I started meditating, I slowly came to understand what my problem was. My overactive mind had put a lock on my feelings. My mind was addicted to thinking, understanding and analysing, and this was proving to be as deadly an affliction as any substance abuse. Through my spiritual practice, I slowly learned to open myself to the heart, and I am still in that process.

I began exploring my spirituality, discovering an inner world filled with very high quality feelings, like love and inner calm. I've learned that, although it is very important to bring understanding to the way we live our life, it is even more important to keep that balanced with simply *being* and to stay in touch with that inner world of wonderful feelings. When the heart and the head work well together, you *become* happy. You don't have to *do* anything to be happy. You just *are*. Everything slows down, becomes real and meaningful, and your interaction with life becomes significant. You think less and you love God. This is an important key. God comes into your life.

I actually never thought much about God in this life. When I understood that part of the meditation course I wanted to take with the Brahma Kumaris included the subject of God, I told the teacher that I hoped we could skip that part. The whole idea of God made me uncomfortable and I seriously considered quitting the classes. That is a pretty amazing way to begin a journey that's brought me to where I am today - someone who considers God the kingpin of her life, the 'card up her sleeve', that is enabling her to become a better person. My relationship with God has become the most important focus of my life, one that I'm still in the process of developing, because I now know that, for me, it is the basis of happiness.

My experience and understanding of God is that He is the source of all these healing, value-based, fulfilling feelings that we want to have in life. Feelings are a kind of energy and there are two containers holding these energies. The soul is one such 'container', and even more so is the Supreme Soul, God. For me, a relationship with God means to belong to that container, to behold that container, to avail myself of all that is contained within that One and in this way become fulfilled. This means to become contented, and contentment makes you a very effective participant in life, because it makes you an easy and constant giver. You can't give what you don't have.

Despite my initial reluctance to entertain the idea of God, I was very fortunate to have a profound experience of Him in the earlier part of my spiritual studies. That was the missing piece for me – the experience. From that moment on, I knew what I needed to do in order to make my life meaningful and significant. I had to understand Him, experience Him and become like Him. My experience of Him is teaching me that this is what is missing in the world. We have all forgotten whose children we are. Too many of us have distanced ourselves from our heritage of divinity. What child wouldn't like to be like his parent, especially if the parent is a model of greatness? And surely this great Parent would like His children to become like Him.

The newness I found in the Brahma Kumaris is the strength that enables me to care and share in a way that sidesteps emotional pain and suffering, so that I never reduce my embrace of life. Because we have all been hurt by love, many of us run from it. Spirituality injects power into our ability to care, making it safe and natural.

The desire to care and share comes from the need to have relationships that connect us heart to heart, soul to soul, and I believe that relationships like this are achievable. Not because two unfulfilled souls come together in a complementary way, but rather as a result of the union of two beings who have learned to stand on their own and who are both fulfilled and contented through spiritual self-governance. For that, we need God, because His wisdom and support is the seed of our becoming whole.

At this time, the world needs the qualities of nurturing and mothering and so I am glad to be who I am at this extremely delicate time. I am a woman, which enables me to act from these caring principles in an unthinking, natural way. I am a child of God, which means that I deeply want to become like my spiritual Father and help in His task of bringing back goodness.

CELEBRATION

"I thought a lot about the relationship between a perfect complete man and a perfect complete woman. I think their relationship is a celebration of each other's part, light and free. When I recognised the difference between love and attachment, I wasn't prepared to live in falsehood any more."

Maureen
Special Placement Teacher
Australia/Hong Kong

I HAD A good childhood and started off without any deep prejudices. Because of that, I thought that my own change would happen a lot quicker than it has. I see other people who have absolute hatred or no self-respect. To change is not an easy process and I think it takes a very healthy spirit to bring it about. On the other hand, it's not just a matter of hard work; it's more a matter of deep realisation, which is where spirituality comes in.

There is a deep core belief in raja yoga that is fundamental - that the eternal and original nature of the self is purity, love and peace; something very positive. As soon as you believe this and then tap into that original state, transformation starts happening very quickly.

Realisation is not an intellectual thing. I have met people practising raja yoga who are very simple and not highly educated, yet they are transforming very quickly. It is really a matter of being willing to do the work and make the transition. For a lot of people, transformation is not even on their agenda.

I do feel that I change every day. I don't think there is a day that goes past without having some kind of insight or realisation. Even more than that, change is taking place in my *sanskars* – tendencies deep within the soul that reveal themselves in my personality and behaviour.

When my husband and I were practising Buddhism, we were very serious about it. We even thought about becoming a monk and nun, but, actually, in two years of serious practice,

I hardly changed at all, except to a small, superficial degree. For example, I became a vegetarian.

I didn't have the power to transform myself, because I felt that it was I who was having to change myself. But since I experienced the relationship with God, in raja yoga meditation, there has been the feeling that I have a lot of help and power coming my way that enables me to make the changes. Basically, it is because of the love that I experience and, when there is love, I can do anything.

I was practising Buddhism, so I didn't believe in God. Even the word God was a big turn-off for me when I did the course in raja yoga. During the second lesson, which is about God, I actually experienced everything that was shared in the guided meditation. I experienced incredible love and peace coming from somewhere and someone, and it was very clear that it wasn't coming from me. So although I didn't want to accept God, I wanted more of that experience and every time I meditated I got that experience.

I think it's the same God for all religions, but people experience and express different qualities of God. I don't think this world could accommodate more than one God! People who experience God, rather than just believe in God, share the same feeling of love, of beauty, of a very gentle presence - a very warm and close feeling.

Raja yoga comes originally from India, but I didn't really mind that because I can adapt to any culture - it's a matter of spirituality. I think that wherever there is spirituality, what we share and experience is very similar. I don't think there is a lot of difference between people who are on the spiritual path, whether they be Buddhist, Christian or Muslim. Working with an interfaith organisation, I interact with people of different faiths. Many of them are busy getting married and are very involved in the world, whereas in raja yoga we are very focused on changing ourselves. That's a high priority in my life, which I don't see to the same level in other people. It takes a lot of power and I believe that it's only God's power that enables me to do it, and if I don't experience the connection with God, I lose the power.

Probably the one change that I notice the most is the emotional independence that I have achieved. I used to be an extremely emotional person and, when I saw someone suffering, I would cry. For two years, I worked on balancing passion with tranquillity. I didn't want to lose my passion, but I didn't want to be disturbed and upset either. Now I get involved in things because of my passion, but I am able to balance it with tranquillity and also keep my mind clear, without disturbing emotions taking over. This helps me to discriminate.

I have a lot of mercy, but sometimes it becomes attachment. With attachment, you want love from someone, rather than giving unconditional love. That neediness is a lack of self-respect. When I am full, then I am not needy, because I am complete. When I am not complete, naturally there will be a lack of self-respect. When I recognised the difference between love and attachment, I wasn't prepared to live with falsehood any more.

I've thought a lot about the relationship between a perfect complete man and a perfect complete woman. I think their relationship is a celebration of each other's part - light and free. It's like exquisite theatre or poetry.

When two people are complete, there is no ownership or dependency. Ownership is about wanting to control and dependency can include manipulation and dishonesty. We are not even aware that we are doing this.

Women have been brought up to be dependent and to feel that we need someone to take care of us, someone to be there.

It is an illusion; we don't need it, because everything we need is in ourselves. It's definitely necessary for women to realise their own power and to empower themselves spiritually. The world won't change until women wake up and realise that they are equal. When men recognise that equality and come into partnership with women, they will transform automatically and naturally.

LOVE

"I always believed God to be my Father, but I had very deep experiences of God as my Mother. As a practical result of this deep feeling of spiritual, motherly love, I lost all my fear and pain of loneliness and felt completely accepted by God. I knew that my search had ended."

Moira
Surgical Nurse
Argentina

WHEN I WAS twenty-three, I left Argentina for a world tour. I didn't know exactly where I was going and for how long. I was not clear on what my search was all about, but I wanted something different. My life, as it was, wasn't working for me. I always felt unfulfilled in my relationships, because my friends could not reach my real self; and I did not know myself at all. When someone said he wanted to marry me, I thought that would be such a boring life. I could not see myself in such a limited way. I always had a strong feeling that I was a person who belonged to the world. The world was mine. No way could I go into the small world of a family life with the same daily routine. I had to find another kind of life and another kind of love.

I toured Europe and spent some time in Greece. I had read a book by Hermann Hesse called Das Glasperlenspiel about an elite group of thinkers and I searched everywhere for that place and those people. Where were these people who knew what I wanted to know?

In Egypt, whilst in the museum of Cairo, I decided that I didn't want to be engaged in the past any more. I had studied museum administration and believed in culture, but I also felt the emptiness of it. Everything was so dead and belonged to the past. There was nothing of the future.

After a year of travelling, I finally reached India. I was very tired and at first I went to the south, to Goa, to rest on the beach. There was so much noise in my head and I was desperately longing for peace. I remember sitting on the beach and feeling such an agony in my heart; such a pain of loneliness. Then all of a sudden, I heard a voice telling me, "Just wait!" This voice was very soothing and I knew that I didn't have to worry any more about where to go. For me, my lack of direction had created so much tension.

I was on my way to Nepal to stay in a Buddhist monastery, but whilst still in India, I came across the headquarters of the Brahma Kumaris in Mount Abu, Rajasthan. When I arrived there, I had the strong feeling that I had found the place and the people I was searching for. My journey was over.

In their silence room, I looked at the picture of Brahma, the founder, and I suddenly realised that it had been his voice that I had heard on the beach. I could connect the voice with the face. I accepted Brahma instantly. To me, he was not a guru, but my spiritual father.

Entering Madhuban, the headquarters of the Brahma Kumaris, was like entering a different world. Travelling around the world on my own, I was often hassled by men. Here, the men in their white clothes were not like that. They were very clean, although they were working so hard in different departments. I used to sit on the swing, looking at them thinking, "These are not men, these are angels." I felt that I belonged to these people and I immediately wanted to change my clothes and wear white like everyone else.

I took a course in raja yoga. When I heard about the soul, as an immortal and eternal being, it made a lot of sense to me. I realised that I was a soul. This gave me an explosion of freedom. Argentina has such an image-orientated culture. You have to be beautiful, slim and smart.

I always knew that I wasn't only that image or body, but what I actually was, I didn't know. My search was just trying to understand what my life was all about; to get a sense of meaning. Understanding myself as a spiritual being was my first attainment.

Coming from ego, I identified myself with toughness and aggression. I had a very bossy character and I had to pay a high price, in terms of hurts to my ego, as a result of this identity. I struggled a lot, because I identified myself with my roles. I had a very strong set of beliefs and tried to fulfil stereotypes. I was always comparing myself with others and, in this way, caused myself a lot of pain.

Slowly, I started to realise that I had my own space. I did not have to manipulate situations or to show off in order to prove myself. The real self does not have to be proved. Being myself meant dying to many aspects of my old self, letting go of everything that I was not, so that my divine personality emerged.

I also very easily accepted the knowledge of God, the Supreme Soul, because I had always been a believer in God. I came to know that raja yoga was about the union with God. In my relationship with God, my first experience was one of instant protection. I always believed God to be my Father but I had very deep experiences of God being my Mother. After a long meditation, I would even feel that a mother was literally holding me. As a practical result of this deep feeling of spiritual, motherly love, I lost all my fear and pain of loneliness and felt completely accepted by God. I felt that God had conquered my heart and I was not alone any more. I knew that my search had ended. I had found the other kind of love. To me, true love means just *being* and allowing others to *be* too, just as God just *is* and allows us to *be*. That's the deepest expression of love.

VICTORY

"In a spiritual life you have to challenge your weaknesses to gain victory over them. I had deep negativity within me and a critical view towards others. I realised that most of the negative things I saw were a reflection of my own negativity. I went into my subconscious and merged the shadow of my soul into my perfect form."

Meera
Educational Trainer
Germany

I WAS LOOKING for love, for a heart experience. I believed in God and also had love for God, but I never had the faith that God could also be my Beloved, because I didn't feel it in my heart. I had a very religious upbringing in Christianity, but in the church there wasn't the openness to discuss these things. When I was sixteen, I spent a lot of time with my friends discussing questions like, "Who is God?" and "Who am I?" We also talked about the world and imagined how it could be. Although we had a great time talking about it, it was only the joy of the intellect, without a heart experience.

So, I started searching. I practised different kinds of yoga and later also took up transcendental meditation. My achievements in meditation were experiences of light and peace, relaxation and detachment. But after some years, I found that there wasn't any further development in my experiences.

Then I came across the Brahma Kumaris and was fascinated by the atmosphere of the meditation centre. The knowledge about the soul, God and the world around me attracted me very much. I had never found a description of God before and no-one had ever told me that I could have a real, personal and direct relationship with Him.

When I started to practise raja yoga meditation, my heart seemed to open and immediately there was a deep experience. Before, I felt that my feelings were covered and that I couldn't reach them or be in touch with them. Through the meditation, I made contact with the core of my being, the source of all my beautiful feelings. It was truly a love experience; but not only love, I also experienced bliss and happiness. I was totally absorbed in that love and I felt that a harmonising took place between my head and my heart.

I began to develop a relationship with God. At first I enjoyed God as my Friend. It was a very sweet relationship, feeling Him on my side. I could talk to Him and, when I was having problems, I was able to catch His answers. I could feel His response. He also inspired me to write beautiful poetry. If you don't know God and you don't know that He is a source of love and only love, you may also think that He punishes. Because of this belief there will always be a distance between you and Him. In this love relationship, I always feel safe and protected.

When I got older, my relationship with God became more mature. He was more like a companion and of course that also brought responsibilities with it. But I soon realised that by having a partnership with God, these responsibilities are shared.

What I found in raja yoga was deep security, something that I had missed in my life. I didn't know my talents or myself and, as a result, I had no faith in myself at all. Through my spiritual practice, I gained self-respect, self-confidence and courage. I will never lose hope, no matter what happens.

In a spiritual life, you have to challenge your weaknesses to gain victory over them. You interact with people you wouldn't necessarily choose to be with, but you find you are able to deal with them in a positive way and this has been a great learning process for me. It wasn't always easy, but it taught me how much resistance there was within me and how much negativity was hidden there, with a very critical attitude towards others. In my mind, I was constantly commenting on the things that other people were doing. I would observe them and then judge them negatively. I had to keep making a conscious decision to be happy or I would have become lost in that negativity. That would then have resulted in the loss of my power and my happiness. I so much wanted a happy life.

I began to observe my behaviour and saw that in many situations, it was as though I was using a razor-blade with which to judge others. I had such a sharp eye, and yet I knew that it was I who had to change my perspective towards the person or the situation. In my experiments, I discovered that I was attached to this way of observing and analysing people. It was as if, by seeing the person's weaknesses and faults, I gained something through it.

I realised that most of the negative things I saw were a reflection of my own negativity. Yes, perhaps there was negativity in someone, but the fact that I was seeing it added to my own negativity. I then decided to go deep into my subconscious, the cellar of the soul, in order to find out why I was behaving in such a manner. I became my own therapist. Before I went into my subconscious, I adopted my perfect light form and also made God my companion. I said to myself, "No matter what you are going to see, just remain in a complete stage of love." It was such a deep experience that all the sorrow of the past came in front of me and I cried a lot, but throughout, I remained conscious of my light form. Finally, I merged the shadow of my soul into my light form and said, "You are me and I am you. We are not separated any more."

It was an incredible experience. As if I knew my enemy and consciously made him my friend so that he could not steal my power any more. During this experiment, I based my consciousness on how God sees me in my perfect form, as His child, pure and complete.

I think I have been perfect at some point in time. Part of my spiritual practice is to regain this perfect form and to experience myself as a perfect being. The awareness of perfection chases away all the shadows from the soul; but without God, that wouldn't be possible. To come to the core of my real self, this perfect being, is only possible with God. In the Bible, it is said that God created man in His own image. I would like to become like God.

Within the Brahma Kumaris, you can see that women have achieved real feminine qualities like generosity, mercy, understanding, wisdom and many powers. On the other hand, they also possess powers like determination, judgment and discrimination, which are said to be masculine. The men within the organisation have developed their feminine side more and it's beautiful to see that they are so lovely and gentle - true gentlemen. You can really see a new manhood here. When we all reach this balanced and complete stage, a new world will emerge for us because, it is said, world transformation takes place through self-transformation. When we share spirituality and divine qualities with one another, this dream will come true.

FAITH

'After ten years of marriage I found myself left without a home, no work, no money and with three children. I refused help from my family and from the government, because I knew that God would help me. And He did.'

Felicity
Community Care Worker
UK/Ghana

I HAD BEEN searching for God since I was seven and, at a very young age, my aim was to become like Mother Theresa, helping poor people in the name of God. Whenever I heard the church bell ringing, I would be the first person to go to church, because I knew that one day I would find God. I was brought up in Ghana as a very strict Christian and I did a lot of praying and also fasting to purify my body. When I came to England, I lost it all, but promised myself that I would go back to religion and to God. However, that didn't happen until I was twenty-five.

I was a very introverted person who didn't mix well with other people. I was always alone, sitting in a corner daydreaming and asking myself questions like, "Who am I? Why am I here? What is this life meant for?" Although I came from a very good and wealthy family, I wasn't happy with my life. I often went to the library, looking for God in the holy and philosophical books. But I couldn't find Him there and I became full of stress.

I had to give up my search for God because, although I would have preferred to stay single, my family, friends and relatives forced me to get married at the age of twenty-eight. Marriage, men and I, never really matched and, soon after my marriage ceremony, I realised that I had made the biggest mistake in my life. After ten years of marriage, I found myself left with no home, no work, no money and with three children. I refused help from my family and from the government, because I knew that God would help me. And He did. Help came from all corners.

After the break up of my marriage, I became a vegetarian and decided to be celibate. And so my search for God began again. I had a series of visions and dreams. In one of them, I saw a man and woman sitting cross-legged, dressed all in white. I also saw a pot of gold, which, for me, symbolised that golden times were ahead.

I travelled to India and liked it very much. I thought I would find God there. I went with my children and stayed with Sai Baba for seven and a half weeks until I realised that he wasn't the one I was looking for. He was a very nice man and very kind to me, but I didn't find God.

At one point, I was extremely ill and stayed in bed for six weeks. One day, I was lying in bed and, all of a sudden, I saw rays of light streaming down on me. It was like gold dust that came down. The experience lasted for about ten minutes and two hours later I was back to life again.

One of my friends, who is a highly respected medium, told me several times that she saw a father figure around me. She said it was someone who had been guiding me since I was a little girl. She also said, "He is going to show himself soon." A few months later, I came home feeling very unhappy because I still hadn't found what I was looking for. As I came in, I saw the light image of a male standing in the doorway. I stared at him for minutes, not saying a word. It was a very powerful experience, but I didn't know who this man was.

Some time later, a friend of mine told me about raja yoga and invited me to come to the meditation centre of the Brahma Kumaris. The moment I walked through the door, it was as if someone said, "Welcome my child," and I knew that I had found what I had been searching for.

After the course, I experienced vision after vision. I saw scenes of my golden future, the beautiful new creation of nature and science, and I remembered the dream about the pot of gold and the yogis dressed in white.

Together with my children, I came to the centre and we all studied there for the first five years, seven days a week, twice a day. The children have stopped now, but they still have faith in this spiritual path. They say that when they have finished what they are doing, they will come back. My daughter studies at the school of journalism and public relations, one son studies art and graphics and the other one music. Each one of them has had very powerful spiritual experiences, which they cannot forget.

My own special experiences also continued. Early one morning, I was sitting in meditation and heard a voice in my mind that said, "Whole night meditation." Three times it was repeated. I said, "Okay", took off from work and sat in silence during the day and night. In the early morning I 'heard' that my daughter had had a very severe car accident while she was driving home from a friend's house, but that she didn't have a single scratch. I was still sitting in meditation when my daughter came in. I knew what had happened to her because at the exact moment of the accident – twelve o'clock sharp – I had the very strong feeling that something was wrong. I knew at the time that I had to stay in meditation in order to spread peaceful and powerful vibrations. I asked her, "Are you alright?" and she replied, "You know, don't you?" The police had said to her, "Your God must be a very powerful God for you to still be alive."

Now, I always feel very protected by God and I don't experience any danger or sorrow. I work with mentally ill people, which is hard work, but being with God makes it all easy. Some people behave very violently towards the other staff, but they never harm me.

I believe there is only one God for all people, but many do not know whether it is Allah, Christ or Buddha. I tell people that God doesn't have a human body, but that He is a pinpoint of light. Deep down inside, they know it is true.

You can only reach God by having a true heart and for that you need three things: complete love, deep faith and surrender, and a pure, clean and clear intellect.

For me, there is only one true guru and that is God. In a relationship with the Supreme Soul or God, everything is included and all my desires are fulfilled. There is love, peace and happiness in my life. Once you connect with God, soul to soul, everything is yours.

This union has an enormous effect on our world. We have been talking about brotherhood for years and years and we are all longing for unity. But not until we all realise that we are souls, children of the same God, can there be that love and respect for one another.

It's God's duty to bring peace to a peaceless world that is full of degradation. The transformation of the human world has already begun, but it will still take time before the new creation is completed.

UNIQUENESS

"I like to keep the balance between truly being myself and at the same time being with others without losing my uniqueness. The more I dissolve my ego, the more I will put others in front, and help them to find their own uniqueness and beauty."

Anna
Teacher of Philosophy and Greek Literature
Egypt/Greece/Lebanon

I CAN IDENTIFY my spiritual awakening as a very specific moment in which I had a deep realisation or vision. It was a clear understanding, or very real experience, of a being that has no physical body like us, but is a perfect being of light.

This being is unchangeable and beyond all the changes in our world. You may call this being God or Truth, but what I felt was love and a deep understanding of who I really am. I was probably having a realisation of God. I realised that God is someone who is always there; someone who could understand me better than I could understand myself.

After this realisation or vision, I was flying with joy. It was something that logic cannot describe. If I hadn't experienced it myself, I wouldn't have believed other people telling me about it. I had very deep clarity in my intellect, without actually thinking, and it felt like a gift given to me. I understood my eternity and my eternal nature, something that liberated me from my fear of death.

Death was a big issue for me because I lost my mother when I was eight years old. Her death had given me the feeling that there was absolutely nothing that had any value to it, because sooner or later we had to die anyway. That fear of death completely left me and I felt relieved, free and happy.

People around me could also see a difference in me and they saw a glow or a pure energy vibrating. I was able to see things in a more universal way and my love for others was no longer restricted to a limited number of people. I could feel that all the people of the whole world belonged to me and I belonged to them and that gave me an experience of true contentment. Everything I have done in my spiritual life after this spiritual experience has been based on this deep and very genuine, true understanding. My aim is to go beyond the limitations of my physical identity and to experience myself as a whole personality, as a spiritual being.

There are very deep, subtle aspects of our personality that we are not aware of, but that need transformation. For instance, ego limits the real self. I like to keep the balance between truly being myself and at the same time being with others, without losing my uniqueness. The more I am able to dissolve my ego, the more I will put others in front and help them to find their own uniqueness and beauty.

To know your own uniqueness and beauty makes you very strong and pure and you start attracting others like a magnet, without needing anything yourself. Because this 'giving' consciousness is pure and without expectation, it doesn't trap others, but liberates them instead. When I am really deep into my spiritual journey and have discovered my own beauty and uniqueness, I won't trap others. When I experience myself and my own freedom, I want others to experience the same. The transformation of my ego has not yet finished, but I can already see how life can be without 'me' being the centre of it. A 'we' consciousness has so much more beauty than an 'I' consciousness.

I am one of those people who doesn't like groups. I never liked belonging to a political party or a religious group. Although I am a Christian and, as a young child, used to go to church, I somehow didn't want to belong to it. I couldn't understand how religions or groups of spiritual people could lay claim to the truth. I always thought that truth was universal.

What I like about the philosophy and knowledge of the BKs is that I am able to go beyond any label or limited identification. This creates a spiritual person, who is ultimately beyond any title, just being the essence of myself. When I am absorbed in this unlimited experience, I am beyond a group, personal identity and titles. I am completely free. This knowledge comes from India. It had to come from somewhere, so why not from India since it's a very attractive and spiritual place? The more I go to the essence of it, the more I pull other people to their essence and help them to go beyond their limitations.

The essence is love. Consciously and unconsciously, people feel this pull to go to the essence of life, whether they call God

'Allah' or 'God'. Whatever religion people practise, it may be Christianity or Islam, I do not want them to leave that and start following a new religion. I only want to share beautiful moments with them; moments of happiness and love related to the deepest part of themselves. I tell them that, for me, God is a perfect being. One of His qualities that I like is that of being selfless and constantly new. God is the one who always responds in the best way ever, so there is newness all the time. Everyone wants to experience God, whatever He might be called in whichever religion. When there is an experience, words finish.

Spiritual service means to do things in their purest form, constantly out of love and not out of attachment to or identification with your ideas, your knowledge, your philosophy or your group. Only when I am detached and pure, can I be sensitive to other people's need. To me that's true service.

INDEPENDENCE

"I do not have to rely on human support any more. This is something that is possible when you are close to God. I came to know God and learned to have all relationships with Him. I am living with God and I experience Him as my Companion. It is just God and me."

La
Account Director, International Advertising Agency
Thailand

GOD HAS ALWAYS been present in my life. He lived with me in my mind. Yet still, I had this deep yearning to meet God, but I didn't know Him or how to turn to Him. I was waiting for someone to introduce Him to me. I thought that if God really and truly exists, I should be the one to know about it. I didn't make any effort for it, because I trusted that God would know that He had to introduce Himself to me.

In Buddhism, they do not speak about God. The word that represents God is 'truth'. Although my parents lived in a country where people practised Buddhism, they were very liberal minded and allowed me the freedom to practise whatever I wanted to. I was attending a Catholic school at that time and so I was also exposed to their ideas.

I was searching for truth, because I knew that truth had to become practical in my life. It should be so powerful that I wouldn't be deceived by my negative feelings. I wanted to be true to myself and to others. I knew intuitively that once truth comes into your own life, you would easily and naturally be truthful to others.

The philosophy I was exposed to in my married life in Japan was that there were three things for which you had to strive: good food, a good house and good clothes. However, I felt that I needed something more than just these material comforts. In Buddhism, they talk about renunciation, but I didn't feel that to be very practical. I didn't want to leave my family or be dependent on a system that didn't allow me to earn my own money. That kind of liberation from responsibility didn't suit me. I wanted to integrate spirituality into my day-to-day life, both in my family as well as in my professional life.

My spiritual awakening took place in Tokyo where I lived for three years. I had a serious problem with my thyroid and was looking for solutions. I went to a lecture about vegetarianism and changed my diet. My husband didn't enjoy the changes and though he tried to understand my choice, he just couldn't. That didn't stop me from being a vegetarian, which was an unusual thing in my culture. In Eastern tradition, it is women who have to please men, so I was lucky that my husband was willing to please me and respected my choice. I also knew that just as the body needs healthy and pure food, so does the soul. I thought that perhaps meditation would help me to improve my health and I started practising raja yoga meditation. With this method of calming my mind, I managed at one point even to stop taking medication.

Raja yoga teaches me how to think in a positive way and my whole lifestyle has changed very naturally and automatically. Raja yoga isn't a dogma, a theory, or something from the scriptures. It is a practical reality based on truth and I learned how to implement truth into my life. I came to understand that truth is a power with which I could face my own falsehood, in a gentle manner. Negativity, which is equal to falsehood, damages our minds and blocks our intellect. When there is still falsehood or negativity within me, I can easily be hurt by others and will also hurt them.

It is hard work to remove prejudice from my thinking. I learned how to make the mind co-operative with the intellect, so that a deep change could take place within my personality. I became someone who was able to share unconditional happiness with others on the basis of my own happiness. The only thing I needed was to be courageous and face all situations. I now trust my love and good wishes to help me handle any obstacles.

I have developed total independence and do not have to rely on human support any more. This is something that is possible when you are close to God. Through raja yoga, I came to know God and learned to have all relationships with Him. I am living with God and I experience Him as my Companion. It's just God and me.

God has prepared me without my knowing it. He has a plan in mind for the world and has made me an instrument for it.

To me, God is the embodiment of truth and there is nothing else that I would like to share in my life. I have such a strong commitment to God, to be a messenger of truth, that nothing can come in my way. God wants to have full cooperation, without any hesitation or objection from my side. It is not only for the sake of humanity that the message of truth has to be spread, but also for my own benefit. By being an instrument of God, I receive upliftment. Understanding that God is the one who allows everything to happen has made me humble and able to go beyond the fruit of my actions. At the same time, it has given me a lot of spiritual strength.

FREEDOM

"The biggest change that has happened within me so far, is the ability to be on my own on an inner level without waiting for somebody else to make me happy or give me something. That neediness of the human spirit, that's gone."

Sister Jayanti
Director, Brahma Kumaris
UK and Europe

I WASN'T INTERESTED in the subject of God, because I had heard so many conflicting stories about God in the East and the West. I thought I could postpone the question of God's existence or non-existence till the end of my life, when I had more time to look at it. But once I had the answer to the question, "Who am I?" it immediately led me to the experience of God. Just as you seek relationships with others on a human level, in the same way when the soul becomes aware of its own original spiritual identity, it is automatically drawn to the experience of connecting with the Divine.

As I studied these unique teachings and practised the meditation, my experiences were so beautiful and powerful that I decided to become a Brahma Kumari and share this information with others. The knowledge I was being taught answered absolutely every single question I had at that moment, but also it opened up further horizons and dimensions that I had not even thought about.

This change of awareness and my new identity brought self-esteem that allowed me to start opening and my inner beauty to shine. A state of cleanliness, in which there isn't anything negative or wasteful touching me, comes through raja yoga, what I would describe as the relationship of love of the soul with the Supreme Soul. If I am still pulled by the pleasures of the physical senses, then I am trapped by the consciousness of the body and that becomes a huge barrier that doesn't allow me to reach God.

The result of having a relationship with God is fulfilment, transformation, the releasing of one's own inner potential and receiving the treasures that one has always wanted. Once I discovered that relationship with God, I began to play with it and develop many different facets that really gave me the possibility of exploring new relationships with people around me.

The biggest change that has happened within me so far is the ability to be on my own on an inner level without waiting for somebody else to make me happy or give me something. That neediness of the human spirit, that's gone. I can now be alone anywhere in the world and yet not being afraid, knowing that I have everything that I need or I can access anything that I need. Anybody on a spiritual path learns to tap into their own inner power and to be independent in the true sense of the word, without dependency on anyone. To me that's real freedom.

When Brahma Baba founded the institution, he entrusted all his finances to a group of twelve young women. He surrendered his property and they became the trustees who were responsible for organising everything within the community. In a very practical way, he set up an organisation run by women. Brahma always wanted women to play the foreground role, so that the imbalance in society could be restored to a state of balance and justice, by giving women the opportunity to be teachers and leaders. This is why he called the organisation, Brahma Kumaris World Spiritual University.

Like everywhere in the world, the organisation cannot function just with women. The aim is transformation of the self and transformation of the world, so it is a question of a partnership with men. This affirmative action allows women to have the role that society has denied them for many centuries.

Within our organisation, the percentage of people who are surrendered and actually live at centres full time is about 80% women to 20% men. Among those who come to the centres to study the teachings and who also help in all the different activities, yet still have their own home and live with their own family, the proportions would be 60% women and 40% men.

People like to be in a position of being wanted and needed. Here the women don't want anything from men, so the men have to find a new role, in which they are able to look women straight in the eye with equality.

Women also tend to fall into old patterns of behaviour. On one side there is the search for freedom, and I think that is the innermost quest for most souls, but on the other side there is the old pattern and the old paradigm. One needs to look at the self very carefully to sort that out.

Men are often competitive, with an ego that creates a power struggle. Within our organisation, a beautiful fact is that since 1969, when the founder passed away, the leadership roles have been in the hands of two women. One of them passed away in 1983 and after that it was a group of three women who were entrusted. I find the relationship between these women, the first group of two and the later group of three, is of such mutual respect and regard that there has never ever been a trace of a power struggle at all. Each one of them is content and fulfilled within themselves, through their own personal relationship with God. It is very easy for these women to be part of a team. They find it very natural to co-operate and share their skills together.

Once I was able to have yoga, I found that my ability to interact with people changed overnight. I was so timid; I couldn't speak to three people. But what has also happened through the years is that my tendency of having likes and dislikes, and of forming opinions about people, has gradually disappeared. Today I feel very confident and, in a very genuine way, it's possible for me to connect on a very deep level with any person, whoever they may be.

LIGHTNESS

"I want to become an angel. To me an angel is someone who gives blessings through the eyes, the mouth and even through the body. An angel gives lightness to others and makes them realise that they are of great value and importance. Angels are the helpers of God. That's what I want to be, the right hand of God."

Chiharu
Office Assistant
Japan

I ALWAYS BELIEVED in God, but didn't practise any religion, apart from some worshiping in the temples and shrines. I knew that God existed and thought that if I went to the temple and donated some money, God would make me into a good person. Although I had money, friends and a good home, there was no fulfilment in my life. I had the feeling that everything in life was perishable, whether it was a party, happiness or a relationship. I knew it would always end and I felt lonely and insecure. One minute there was extreme happiness and the next minute I felt sorrowful and depressed, knowing that it wouldn't last for long. It was then that I said to God, "Now you must fulfil my real desire."

I wanted to get to know myself and so I read several spiritual books in order to find the answers to my questions about life. Then in Disneyland, I met a sister from the Brahma Kumaris who told me about raja yoga meditation. That meeting turned out to be the start of my new life.

I accepted all the knowledge that they shared with me at the meditation centre without a single doubt. It was like food for the soul. I used whatever was said in the lessons and experimented with the universal principles of truth that I was hearing. Truth only comes from God and it was on the basis of that truth that I changed. Each day, I had many realisations and, in four months, I became a totally different person.

Without anyone telling me, I always knew that to get up in the early morning was a good thing to do, but somehow could never manage it, because I had no power. By simply putting this suggestion into practice, I discovered the benefit of it and am now able to do it easily. The world is so different at 4 o'clock in the morning, so serene and silent, because everybody else is asleep at that time. I didn't know this silent world before.

Every morning, I went to class at 6am before going to the office, even though I felt very tired and I had other people telling me that I looked tired. But I couldn't stop going there, because spiritually it refreshed me so much.

For the first time in my life, I felt self-acceptance. I had always criticised and corrected others and myself, and because of this negative habit, people didn't like me very much. But the reason I had been critical came from my own feeling of righteousness. "Wrong is wrong", I thought. Deep within myself I knew what was right, but couldn't put it into practice in the right way. I knew that it was better not to get angry, but still I got angry over people's mistakes and then would correct them. I was too "lawful" towards others, pointing out their weaknesses and afterwards would feel so depressed about it. Still, I believed that the inside and outside of people shouldn't be different. Although I thought that I was doing the right thing, I felt sad because of other people's negative responses to me.

Through spiritual insights, and in particular understanding the law of the cause and effect of my actions, and also through long meditations, I had deep realisations about anger and the effect of it. I decided not to become angry any more, nor to react to people's mistakes. My transformation took place on the basis of these realisations. My parents couldn't change me, no person could, but it was God who transformed me and now I know how to connect with Him and have a relationship with Him. What I needed was a spiritual guide and now I've also got a teacher and a spiritual family.

I want to become an angel. To me, an angel is someone who gives blessings, through the eyes, the mouth and even through the body. An angel gives lightness to others and makes them realise that they are of great value and importance. Angels are the helpers of God. That's what I want to be, the right hand of God.

TRUTH

"I have always been searching for my absolute truth, but often found only a relative truth. When I found my absolute truth, it changed my inner being completely. My consciousness changed instantly and my highest personality of purity emerged."

Cecilia
Advertising Executive
Bolivia

I USED TO have a materialistic lifestyle. I could get whatever I wanted and I was what they call in Spanish 'the peanut of the parties', which means that I was present at all of them. Now I live a more simple life, though due to the role I play in Bolivian society, I still wear good clothes, but a more classical look, not the latest fashion. I have people who help me with the cleaning, a chauffeur and a nanny. I also have a nice car, because that's the way I am and that's the role I play in life. But now the difference is that I am not attracted to it or dependent on it. I still go to social meetings, but with the pure desire to serve.

The biggest change that my friends noticed was that I stopped riding horses and jumping. I was good at it, but I felt that it wasn't good to force an animal to do something that was unnatural to him. Now I play tennis instead.

In the beginning, my friends and family did not take me seriously, but now they are respectful. They can see that, after all these years, I am stable in my beliefs. Instead of a glass of wine, they will offer me juice or water. Now, they don't come to talk to me about the latest hairstyle, because they know that I have something different to share with them. Our friendship is deeper and more honest, and we accept each other the way we are.

I became a Brahma Kumari by accident. It wasn't a conscious choice. When a friend of mine invited me to go to the raja yoga centre, I thought that spirituality was the last thing I needed at that moment. Instead of going to the meditation centre, I invited her for a glass of wine and a pizza, but I ended up taking the meditation course that same day. I had never seen myself as a spiritual person, but I was someone who was looking for answers and the knowledge of the Brahma Kumaris answered every question that I had.

I had always been searching for my absolute truth, but often found only a relative truth. When I found my absolute truth, it changed my inner being completely. My consciousness changed instantly and my highest personality of purity emerged. There are many relative truths, but my ultimate truth is the only truth capable of changing me. My transformation is the proof of my absolute truth; otherwise it would just be change, but no real transformation. Perhaps there would be a change in my style of eating, talking, walking and relating to other people, but real transformation only takes place when I am in my absolute truth. It all depends on my state of awareness and my attitude as to whether I am able to live my truth.

For me, it's vital to have a good early morning meditation, because it sets my whole day. It's a good way to keep a high state of consciousness during the day. One has to perform different actions throughout the day in an elevated state of consciousness or it becomes too easy to get influenced or pulled by this material world, in which everything is designed to attract your five senses.

Right from the start, I focused a lot of attention on my early morning meditation. At that time, I was experiencing a love affair with God. I had to sneak out of my bed secretly, in order not to disturb my husband's sleep. It was such a deep romantic encounter with God. I would wake up at two, three or four o'clock in the morning, just to feel the rays of loving energy. My husband got the idea that I was having an affair and I had to admit that, yes, I was having the greatest affair of my life - with God!

Though my husband always respected my decisions, we had a hard time in the beginning. He was concerned about my change of perspective with regards to my new way of living. He couldn't believe that I was now interested in spiritual things, because I had been more into consumerism and material things. He thought that it was just another phase in my life that would pass. When he started to see that I was determined to have a spiritual lifestyle, little by little, he began to accept my decisions.

I explained to him that I needed time to experiment with different things and he accepted my proposal to be celibate for six months. When the six months passed, he wanted to go back to our previous lifestyle, but I just couldn't. I told him that he was free to make any decisions about our marriage. It was after a lot of introspection and reflection that he decided to go along with me. He is a very important person in my life and he is the father of my two children. His ethical and moral standards are very high and that makes him a stable and co-operative person as well.

As the time went by, he accepted my choice completely and I really believe that it must have been God's touching that inspired him.

This absolute truth has opened my mind and heart to such an extent that I now feel love for the whole of humanity, without discriminating between age, culture, race, background or status. My whole point of view has changed. I always considered myself to be a humanistic kind of person, because I had travelled in many countries of the world and come across a variety of cultures. But now I enjoy serving them in one way or another. The awareness of being part of God's plan made me into a true unlimited server.

My highest state of consciousness made it clear to me that the world needs true instruments of God. God has a plan for the world. He wants to rejuvenate souls and change the state of consciousness of the human race; and we, as co-creators, are helping Him. We are changing the world. Can you believe that? There's a silent revolution going on, silent and non-violent, but very powerful.

Most people think that if the world changes, they will also change. But it's the other way round: when I change, the world changes.

SOUL CONSCIOUSNESS

"I am the same person as I have always been and I don't have any intention of becoming a different person. When I am spiritually connected, soul conscious and focused in my practice of meditation, my higher qualities naturally reveal themselves. When I am disconnected and depleted, then naturally any negative qualities are able to express themselves."

Denise
Academic Advisor
India/USA

MY INTEREST IS in God. I don't have an emotional relationship with God as my Father as such. Rather, God is God to me and not so much Father and Mother. I think it's partly due to my being a self-absorbed person and I do not tend to identify myself via particular relationships.

My relationship with God is very intense and other worldly. There is intense love and it is also very silent. It is an eternal awareness. There is a major difference between my sense of existence in a terrestrial sense and my sense of existence above and beyond it, outside of death, outside the world, outside day-to-day life. I feel that I was called by God, personally and very directly, in a visionary way and that I have something to do. It's a calling and so I am doing what I feel is God's work. This life of mine is for a special purpose. I consider myself a revolutionary, not a violent revolutionary, but someone who is involved in bringing about, by spiritual means, a new civilisation, which is being engineered by God.

I live at the Brahma Kumaris headquarters, where there are 1400 of us living and working permanently and about that many again who come for about three to four months at a time. Over and above that, there are thousands of people who spend three to four weeks here every year. I feel it is like a civilisation. It is as if I live in a holy city where all the people are in a natural spiritual practice. So there is an atmosphere from the vibrations and feelings of all the people and that resonance binds us to each other harmoniously.

I like my privacy and I like my solitude and in these surroundings it's possible to have total solitude, to be absolutely alone and be totally responsible for yourself, but at the same time to have a feeling of comfort and security. As a result, I don't have an adversarial relationship with the world.

I have a very active inner life. I don't need anybody, but I enjoy my friendships. I feel connected with people who have my kind of values. Most people like to have a significant other and a circle of close friends. For myself, I came to understand a few years ago that my way, my destiny, is to be a loner. I have a lot of good friends, but I am very much a person on my own. I also have a lot of long-distance relationships in which I am mentally very connected to certain significant people, regardless of them being a few hundred or a few thousand miles away.

I made a definite choice over thirty years to be celibate and not have emotional or sexual involvement. Although I myself am a very passionate and intense kind of person, the sense of my own continuity, my multitude of lives and so on, allows me easily to say, "Well, I will take on family and relationships another time."

My feeling about myself is that I am the same person as I have always been and I don't have any intention of becoming a different person. My feeling though is that when I am spiritually connected, soul conscious and focused in my practice of meditation, my higher qualities naturally reveal themselves. When I am disconnected and depleted, then naturally any negative qualities are able to express themselves. I do not see transformation as before and after, like an advertisement for diet pills or hair restoring lotion, but as a continuous process. There is a discernable accumulation of yoga power of spiritual energy over the years and the self gradually matures. I have an inner conviction that is a very fearless state, I have experienced that I can't be influenced or broken or corrupted or bought. I am my own person and that's a very good feeling; that's my accomplishment of realising myself and feeling my power to the extent that I am satisfied with it.

I don't subscribe to the idea that I am a low, miserable sinner. There isn't anything in my life that I regret. The idea of purification is always associated with a sense of sinfulness. There is another word that I like better, which is transfiguration. This enables me not to be susceptible to any of the things that might be classified as evil. I have had near-death experiences and I found out that I am not fear-based. I am not afraid of death or pain. Pain has probably been my greatest teacher and it continues to be. I think that, for me, purification is to have had sufficient experience, accompanied by the accumulation of spiritual power for personal progress. Purification means you can look at the dark side of yourself or of the world with neutrality.

EQUALITY

"I believe that men and women can be equal when men realise that women require respect too. Both need inner transformation. In my marriage, there is equality between my husband and myself. He gives me a lot of respect and I give the same respect to him. In some aspects he is ahead of me, and in other aspects I am ahead of him. So there is always a balance."

Sister Usha
Vice President, BK Art and Cultural Wing
India

SINCE CHILDHOOD, I have been travelling throughout the world to spread the message of peace and spirituality. I do not see any difference between East and West. Perhaps the West is materialistically more progressive and developed, but everywhere people's inner lives have become empty.

Science has brought so much comfort to our lifestyle, but there is no balance between mind and body, and mind and spirituality. In a material sense, we are advanced, but mentally and emotionally we are still behind. This imbalance causes a lot of stress. Human relationships are very complicated nowadays and bring a lot of inner dissatisfaction. In the western world, people may seek help from psychiatrists and psychologists and, in India, it has now become fashionable to follow courses in positive thinking and stress management. The problems are the same. The root cause of all the problems is negative thinking.

I feel that it's very necessary to combine science and spirituality. When science and silence come together, it will bring more light to our minds. It will bring back peace and purity.

Balance needs to be brought back to many areas of life, and also within our relationships. I believe that men and women can be equal, when men realise that women require respect too. Both need inner transformation. In my marriage, there is equality between my husband and myself. He gives me a lot of respect and I give the same respect to him. In some cases he is ahead of me and in other cases I am ahead of him. So there is always a balance.

Presently I am giving spiritual training to artists to bring back the balance between art and spirituality. An artist, who is spiritually minded, is more introverted and goes into the depth of art and, as a result, the art that they perform is more refined. Their artwork, whether it be a painting, a dance, a song, a sculpture or a fashion design, is performed in such a way that something unique is seen - something completely different from general art. The artist knows how, in a natural way, to give a spiritual touch to his expression of art, which makes the public feel as if it's coming from the Divine. I have worked with a singer, who was number one in India, on the production of a CD made up of special songs. She is a very good singer with a very good voice. I told her that, whilst singing, she should remember God or whoever she believed in, and to sing in such a way as if she was totally lost in that love. She had sung at least a thousand songs before, but after she connected spiritually to God whilst she was singing, everyone who heard those songs, fell in love with God.

Some artists can be self-centred and sensitive, so they need to be treated with all possible care. They often feel that they are not respected, whereas in fact, they are hungry for self-respect. Through spirituality, they come to feel their own self-respect and so do not need to look outside themselves for it. Because of having self-respect, they develop a deep satisfaction about themselves and their artistic life.

Artists who are spiritually touched are very humble and don't run after name, fame or money. In humility lies greatness and, in a very natural way, talent and success comes to them as a present from God. Once I organised a big conference where all the great artists from the Indian film world were present: actresses, filmmakers, musicians, singers etc. In the spiritual environment that we had created, they all became very simple people, in the sense that their ego completely disappeared.

I have seen that same humility in our founder, Brahma Baba. He told us that he was just a student, like us. Everything we did, like washing clothes or cleaning, he did the same. He put women in front and gave them respect. He not only gave them all the material and physical comforts, but inner and spiritual comfort as well. He taught me that it's also important to keep a balance between the material and spiritual. He was also the one who taught me the art of living a family life and yet remaining spiritual.

POWER

"What I enjoy most is the spiritual journey. There has been smooth sailing and there have been rough roads, but it is all a tremendous learning experience that has strengthened the soul. With the help of more experienced people, and by using my spiritual powers, I can reach a state of equanimity."

Vishantie
Civil Servant
Trinidad

SPIRITUALITY FOR ME is a very natural way of being in which I express my true qualities. In my day-to-day activity and in my relationships with others, I interact on the basis of my core values in life. Spirituality and values are interlinked and you cannot separate them. The essence of spirituality is the values. Once you practise the values, automatically your spirituality will emerge. The behaviour and activity of a person, who practises values in his or her life, will be different from someone who doesn't.

Some core values are: love, respect, co-operation and creativity. When it comes to actions, one would have these values as an underlying principle.

I lacked self-respect and it took me a long time to regain it. For me, self-respect is a state of being in which I am stable in the awareness of my true qualities. No matter what one says about me in a negative way, I am not affected, because I know who I am. Knowing my true identity makes me humble, rather than arrogant. Inside I feel great, but in my interactions with other people humility helps. In order to give respect to others, I need to be in the awareness of my true self-respect.

My self-respect is based on my core values and qualities such as love, happiness, purity, bliss and power, knowing that I am a child of God and knowing my role in the whole setting of life. Once I am able to have that consciousness, then automatically these spiritual values will come out in my interaction with others.

With the help of spirituality, I was able to see myself as God sees me. I saw myself through God's eyes. I saw someone who has the potential to become so beautiful, so powerful and so loving; a person who mirrors the personality of God. When I received the knowledge of the soul and God, the Supreme Soul, my quality of wanting to serve society emerged. I wanted everyone to experience the happiness and bliss that comes from a relationship with God. Very naturally, I dedicated my life to this work.

In Trinidad, violence has increased and there are racial problems. People have now started realising that one has to go beyond the physical dimension in order to have a more spiritual solution to problems. We have several groups that pray together and we also have an inter-religious organisation that brings together all religious groups. They do special service, particularly for peace in our country.

What I enjoy most is the spiritual journey. There has been some smooth sailing and there have been rough roads, but it is all a tremendous learning experience which has strengthened the soul. With the help of more experienced people, but also by using my own spiritual powers, I can reach a state of equanimity. I am now able to lend a hand to others very easily when necessary, or even to be a support with my thoughts or through the power of my mind.

Spirituality has enabled me to do what is necessary, while remaining in my own self-respect, and not to have expectations or to make demands of others concerning what I want. Self-respect is a power which has enabled me to remain unaffected by other people and circumstances.

Both men and women need to develop self-respect. It is women, in particular who can bring spirituality back into society. They can bring the spiritual strength of unity into domestic and professional life. Men and women need to view each other with equality and respect. This would be specially beneficially in the world of advertising, where images of women are so often used to promote sales.

In a relationship where the woman starts to change, the situation in the home changes automatically. In the case of an argument or conflict, when a woman or man ceases to react to a situation and shows strength through tolerance instead, a positive atmosphere is created. When a marriage becomes insecure and one partner begins to study spiritual knowledge and apply values in their life, a new relationship can unfold. The peace, love and tolerance that change the atmosphere in the home can save the marriage. Positive change in one partner will have a positive influence on the other.

HEALING

"In the meditation room, I had a deeply spiritual experience
that had a physical feeling, almost a sound, to it. I could feel
it around my throat, then my heart and also in my stomach.
There was a healing taking place... It was like a resolving of
the past and the birth of my true self-respect."

Tamasin
Actress/Paramedic
Australia

I WASN'T BROUGHT up with any religious background at all. I
wasn't christened or baptised. My parents, who followed an
Indian guru called Swami Muktananda, amongst various
other paths and philosophies, wanted to allow me the

freedom to believe what I wished. Between the ages of eleven and fifteen, I searched very intensely for some spiritual answers; although my search goes as far back as I can remember. My burning desire was to find happiness and to bring happiness to others, because I couldn't stand the sorrow in the world. That's what motivated my search. It was my driving force.

I used to sit in my bedroom and say, "I am me, I am me", over and over to myself in an attempt to understand who I was. I used to go to the church down the road to talk to God and I would repeatedly ask Him these same three questions, "Who am I? Why am I me? What makes me 'me'?"

I was interested in the story of Christ and also in Eastern religions, such as Buddhism. I wasn't exactly sure what I was looking for. Somehow I knew that I was a spiritual 'being' and that God was also that, but separate and distinct from me. I used to look at one particular star at night, and I knew that was what God looked like. I also knew that God was a spiritual personality and not omnipresent. I cannot talk about a "spiritual awakening": I woke up many times! I so wanted to understand God, who He was and what He did.

At the time I became a raja yogi, my self-respect was very low. I thought that God didn't love me and I felt completely worthless. I wanted to follow celibacy but couldn't convince my boyfriend. I truly did want to live a pure life, because the emotional entanglement of relationships was causing me so much sorrow.

I never stopped feeling God's presence. I felt Him very quietly loving me, but allowing me to find things out for myself - He has that much regard for my choices and me. I really had to understand how emotional dependency and attachment work.

Slowly, I realised that I couldn't have a fully committed spiritual life, and do spiritual service, if I was in a relationship. Perhaps others can do this, but personally I can't. I then made a decision for lifelong purity and commitment to God. I did this as an adult, in my own right. I was twenty-five, and knew that was what I wanted.

After this experience, I went to Madhuban, the Brahma Kumaris' headquarters in India. While I was there, I felt remorseful about aspects of my previous life because purity was, and is, a big thing for me. But then I kept thinking, "This is the time that the impossible becomes possible", and I also knew that determination was the key to overcoming anything, including my lack of self-respect, my feelings of guilt and my inability to love myself. I truly wanted to transcend my limited personality and to break free from it.

There, in the meditation room, I had a deeply spiritual experience that had a physical feeling, almost a sound, to it. I could feel it around my throat, then my heart and also in my stomach. There was a healing taking place and it was a feeling of erasing the effect of my hurt. It was clear to me that it was God. I knew that it was the return of my determination, because my deepest solitary commitment was to God. It was at this point that I knew I could fulfil His vision of me. It was like a resolving of the past and the birth of my true, unbreakable self-respect.

Before that experience, anything I did didn't seem to work. I just didn't believe that God loved me. I couldn't embrace my divinity. That spiritual experience in India was a huge turning point. From then on, I started to create a foundation of self-respect and I felt that God really accepted and loved me.

After the healing took place, I was more open to my spiritual transformation. I needed to change the way I was talking to myself and so I started doing affirmations related to my true self, "I am strong! I am loved! I am beautiful!" I realised that lack of self-respect is also the habit of getting stuck in the moment and the inability to see the bigger picture. I had kept myself contained and had lived in fear, instead of allowing myself to be free and gracious, full of wonder. I now know and experience that I am a pure soul; an absolutely divine 'being' that is extremely close to God. I had picked up some stuff along the way, but that was part of my journey. God's love melted the shell that kept my beauty hidden and my self-respect low.

It is now possible for me to experience intimacy and deep love with God, with all the romanticism I need. But first I had to make the decision to shut the door to human love - to still have loving relationships, but to stop using human love as the support for my life. In human relationships, I was looking for love, acceptance and the feeling of being special to somebody, but I wasn't experiencing that soul-intimacy. Since I have had the courage and faith to give myself to God alone, I experience God's profound and complete love, along with a much deeper intimacy. I feel that it's all for me alone. With God as my Beloved, the result is that I want to share this love with others in a natural way. With human love, I wanted to keep it for myself, because I was afraid of losing it.

In order to love yourself, you also need the good wishes of other people. Good wishes have an extraordinary power. I used to shut off that power as a way of justifying my lack of self-respect. It's literally by God's love, grace and blessings, and the love and good wishes of my spiritual brothers and sisters that I am here today. I belong to God and God belongs to me.

SELF-RESPECT

"Purity is deeply connected to self-respect. When I lost my virginity, I lost part of my identity. I was always looking to the needs of others, never to what I needed myself. As soon as I took my purity back into my own hands I started to rediscover myself."

Belinda
Administration Manager
South Africa

FOR ME, PURITY is the basis of my spirituality. If I look back over my life, there was always a natural spirituality, but I also know that there was a period of my life when I lost sight of that. It was very much connected to the loss of my purity. I lost my virginity, I lost part of my identity. It must be something very sacred and deeply connected to my sense of identity. When it's lost, so much changes.

I might not have thought directly, "I am impure", but definitely my attitude towards myself changed. The sense of my own divinity was lost. Over a period of time, that brought me further and further down and, of course, society doesn't help. The role of a wife and mother is still, even in the west, a subservient role. It's not put in its rightful place. Being someone's wife, and being a mother, and trying to find fulfilment in those roles, it was almost as if I lost myself - I couldn't see myself at all.

As soon as I mentally took my purity back into my own hands, my attitude towards myself change again. I began to rediscover who I was, to value my own opinion of life and how I felt about the world and its challenges. It was almost as if these things had been swept away somewhere and I had forgotten them. I was always looking to the needs of others, never to what I needed myself. The ability to love and cherish the self is deeply connected to purity.

It was a powerful decision, to lead a pure life, and everything that happened after I had made that decision cleared the path for it to become a reality. I didn't have to go through a lot of upheaval, not within myself, nor from outside either. It was almost as if that thought was so filled with determination that it happened very quickly and very naturally. Soon after I began my spiritual journey, my husband said, very spontaneously, "I suppose the next thing will be that you want to be celibate?" I said, "Yes!" without hesitation and he just seemed to know that there was actually no margin in it. Immediately, I was able to see him in a universal sense. It was easy for me to have a vision of brotherhood and to feel that, "This is my soul brother." It was my first experience of this kind of change, but as my spiritual life developed, I interacted with other men too in a very different way. When my aim was not to find a relationship then my way of interacting and speaking totally changed.

I am not just leading a celibate life, but also practising the consciousness that goes with it. The way I think, what motivates me, my changes in attitude, each impact on the way I interact with the opposite sex. I saw within myself very old habits, especially the subtle games that women play, and of course that doesn't disappear overnight. I found it necessary to watch myself. I saw the manipulation in how I used my feminine side to get my own way, and that was part of the impurity that I wanted to let go of.

Purity is a power that replaces the old way of trying to get things out of people. Purity, for me, is deeply connected to self-respect.

In raising my own daughters, I have tried to help them not to fall into the typical mindset of being a woman in society and the limitations that it can place on women. In my older daughter, I see a sense of freedom. She is not bound by the stereotype that I was bound by. My younger daughter is like a story unfolding. I see that in her own life, she is using the values that we have discussed and experimented with. When you have values, it is like a natural spirituality. If one day they decide to get married and have families, they will be successful, because they have that love for spirituality.

In a way, I am a nun, because my life is dedicated to my pursuit of spirituality and self-discovery, and also to knowing God and feeling close to God. If one is celibate from birth, like nuns, maybe the difference doesn't seem so great, but in my case, having had a family and having played that role, my life feels very different. I have made a choice and I feel a lot of power through making that choice.

I could recognise that mankind has been on a journey throughout all the ages. Perhaps it has been a downward journey, but there have been some wonderful experiences on the way.

When I looked at the world and I saw the state it was in, I began to recognise that the power of purity at this time is very special and necessary. We have had beautiful relationships with God, but never has there been so much negativity and never has it become so difficult to make that connection with God. So to choose this time to lead a pure life - for me, the magic lies in this. It seems to be this kind of courage that attracts God into your life, because you are choosing something unique. And in my case, it was leaving one way of life and taking something new on board. Many people thought it was a loss and were strongly critical, but I had recognised, deep within, that I desperately wanted to make a difference in the world. The moment I heard about the connection between purity and coming close to God, and transforming myself and the world around me, it made so much sense.

Purity is needed to transform the self at a very deep level. I feel that transformation comes from the platform of purity, which allows you to see the beauty of the soul. Without purity, you can see it to a limited extent but not enough to transform in a permanent way. Now I try to look at myself just with my heart and even the parts that I regard as weaknesses, I see in a very gentle way. When I am focusing on my beauty, compassion and gentleness, which are very feminine qualities, I feel them within me. I don't worry about those weaknesses. In their own time, they will change into the colours that I want to see.

As souls, I believe that we have experienced both the masculine and the feminine side of ourselves. Men are also discovering that inner beauty, the feminine, but they also need to look at the masculine within, to see that there is beauty there also.

Recognising their journey and the resulting pain that men have gone through, I feel that they have actually been their own worst enemies. Especially when we look at the stereotypic roles that they have taken on as their assumed strength and then seeing how those roles actually led to a lot of pain. I feel much more compassionate towards men today than I did before.

SELFLESSNESS

"I always loved people, but my love was conditional. I expected the return of it. Spiritual love, however, is altruistic; you just give. It's love that comes from another dimension. These high-quality, loving feelings are what I am now sharing with others."

Mathilde
Nursing Tutor
India/Netherlands

LOVE IS THE main ingredient for any healing, whether it's the mind, the heart, the body or the soul. Without love, no real healing takes place.

It is said that it isn't the medicine that cures the patient, but the hand that gives the medicine. The attitude of a doctor or a nurse makes such a difference when it is loving and filled with sincere attention. I always tell the students that the first injection they must give to the patients is an injection of love. Just go on your round and give everyone a smile. Don't do anything else and that will be the start of the healing process for the day. Healthcare is the art of healing the patient's body and mind. You need an holistic approach to any healing process, where both the healer and the patient are included. The mind and body of the patient have to be ready to heal, and until they are, you can't do much except guide them to that holistic understanding.

I have been in nursing many years and I have always had the desire to add spirituality to my professional life, because I saw how much the patients needed that. It wasn't always easy to integrate the sharing of love when taking blood pressure, because in regular healthcare there has always been a separation between head and heart. Most of us hide our feelings behind our medical mask, even though healthcare workers in general are people who like to help and serve others from their heart. Most of us have the desire to express that spiritual love, but are still unable to do so. Sometimes it's a cultural thing; we are not used to sharing our love with strangers, just like that. Also, in healthcare nowadays there is more work and less time. But the expression of love, or giving of a smile, doesn't cost anything and doesn't require extra time.

You need some courage to be different. I became a different nurse because of my spiritual practice. It took me a few years to be free enough to express love to my patients. I was a very practical person and only went to see someone if there was a need for it, not just for human contact. Now I sit with them, listen with attention and try to empathise with their feelings and experiences.

The basis of loving others is loving yourself and that is something you have to learn. I always loved people, but that love was conditional. I expected the return of it. Spiritual love, however, is altruistic; you just give. It's love that comes from another dimension. In my meditations, I experience spiritual love from God and I fill myself with that love. These high-quality, loving feelings are what I am now sharing with others. In my work, I try to be an embodiment of that unconditional love, because I know it is of great benefit to the patients. Even when they are about to die, your presence and loving vibrations work very positively, even better than fighting for their life with force. As souls, spiritual beings, we are longing for light and for the loving presence of God, especially at the end of our life. The experience of spiritual light is in fact the experience of the dimension where God resides. In my meditations, I have that same experience of golden red light, the symbol of total freedom. When I raise my consciousness and concentrate my mind, I can imagine and experience God, the ocean of light. I see a tiny point of concentrated spiritual light and am able to silently communicate with this supreme being of love.

God is our healer, even when we suffer due to the effect of our own karmic bondages, that is, the effect of our own negative actions. Negativity causes pain, not only on a physical level, but also in our relationships with other people in the form of non-acceptance or jealousy. All kinds of suffering can end with the help of the healing power of God's love.

Some time ago, I woke up in the middle of the night with an enormous pain in my chest. I realised that I had misused my body by working too hard, not being able to say 'no' to people or to my own expectations of myself.

I started to give loving healing power to my heart and said to myself, "It's okay now; with God's love you will overcome this suffering." I was actually healing my pain with the visualisation of that healing energy streaming through my heart.

It is very essential to teach patients how to heal themselves with this method, besides having surgery or taking medicines.

For a few years now, I have been working at the Global Hospital in Mount Abu, India, a place where healthcare and spirituality are integrated. The surgeons here say that they are instruments of God, that they aren't the ones who are doing the surgery, but that it is God who does it through their hands. I also feel that I am an instrument. God's light works through me and I only have to be spiritually aware and connected to God in order to make that happen. I used to lose so much energy during my work, but now I understand that it's because of a lack of self-respect. I used to pray to God, asking for love. Now it's more like communicating with Him in an equal way. I fall in love with God and I like to be in that love-energy all the time, whilst serving and loving other people.

TRANSFORMATION

"Unless I am in touch with my deep feelings, transformation cannot occur. Transformation is not just about changing my thoughts or my way of thinking. True transformation is when I change my way of feeling."

Gayatri
BK representative to UN
USA/Guyana

HINDUISM AND CATHOLICISM were the two religions that influenced the person I was in my earlier days. I was born in the Hindu religion and I also attended a Catholic school when I was growing up. I believe that I was able to appreciate the spiritual dimension of these religions. I was operating from a basic spiritual principle that, at some level in our existence, we stand on common ground.

The greatest happiness that I experienced, what I call a highpoint, was when I entered the meditation centre of the Brahma Kumaris. I was nineteen years old and I saw people from different racial backgrounds sitting and looking at a point of light, that represented God as the focus of their meditation. My happiness came from the realisation that, if there were a God, God would reveal Himself or Herself to us in a way that we could all relate to, regardless of our race, religion or anything else that could be perceived as a difference or a discord in our lives.

I was then able to appreciate the spiritual dimension and significance of many of the stories and rituals that I heard in Hinduism and in Catholicism.

I wear a white sari because it helps to show who I am and the path I have chosen for my life. It's a uniform that the founder of the Brahma Kumaris actually recommended. When people see me in a white sari, they see me as a person who has committed her life totally to spirituality and they also understand that one of the principles by which I live is the principle of purity. I have taken certain vows; one of which is celibacy.

Celibacy is part of a commitment to a larger concept of purity, which includes purity of thoughts, feelings and actions.

In wearing this white sari, I don't intend to put myself in a limited category or in an organisational framework, because even though I belong to the organisation called the Brahma Kumaris, I move in this world as an individual who is working with the collective to bring about world transformation. I understand world transformation to begin with individual transformation, which is my own personal change.

I remember such a moment of immense personal transformation. I was growing up in the country of my birth, Guyana, as a woman who was extremely protected emotionally. I had my father, my uncles from both my father's and mother's sides, and my cousins, and they would always be around us like a protective hand. I was not exposed to anything such as emotional hurt or pain. When I came to the United States and people talked about emotional pain, I couldn't relate to the word 'pain' in this context. For me pain was a cut on your foot, but that pain healed. I could not understand what kind of pain they were talking about. One day, someone was telling me her story and I was listening to it very objectively. She realised that I wasn't empathising at all and said, "You don't have a reference point, do you?" In my mind I thought, "Of course I have a reference point." But I didn't realise the depth of her comment, until a few years later when I had an operation and I was lying in a hospital bed. All of a sudden, it was like an avalanche of panic and an eruption of all my feelings and I thought, "Now I do!" It was a moment of realisation that unless I am in touch with my deep feelings, transformation cannot actually occur. Transformation is not just about changing my thoughts or my way of thinking, but true transformation is when I change my way of feeling. When I feel differently about myself, then I will not feel isolated from the pain of other people. I might not have had a relationship in this particular birth in which I was emotionally hurt, but I might have had it in previous births and that hurt may have been suppressed within me.

When a situation arises in one's life that makes one vulnerable, that is normally seen by the world to be a weakness. But the transformation that occurs within me, at moments of vulnerability, is actual inner strength. When this happens, it expands my capacity to see myself, my relationships and the world differently, on the level of feelings. Vulnerability softens my stronger side and I am able to be a better human being. When I see people in pain, I am able to help them, not only through my words, but also on a level of vibration. It is because of my own transformation that I can offer them strength.

It was relatively natural for me to adopt a life of purity. For me, celibacy is part of the overall concept of purity. I have found that celibacy gives me a lot of self-respect and independence. We tend to define our identity based on what someone else thinks of us, and celibacy allows me to see myself outside the mirror of someone else. This enables me to have equality in my relationship with men. When I look at a man, I see him on many levels - intellectually, emotionally and spiritually - without feeling inferior. I see him as my equal, as a friend or brother. I feel a lot of love for some of the men I have met in my spiritual life, love that comes from a depth of mutual respect. I feel that my men friends see the purity within me as strength in the relationship, which they would like to uphold. What they want from me is my help to sustain their spirituality.

Although women lead the Brahma Kumaris, this organisation is neither about women's supremacy nor about diminishing men. Rather, it is about highlighting the feminine principles in all people in such a way that men can take spiritual power from these principles to bring balance in their lives. This makes them feel better about themselves and enables them to look at women with a vision of equality.

My femininity is being empowered and nurtured by the strength of my relationship with God as my Mother and

Father. The inheritance and the attainments that I take from this relationship mould my personality. I feel that it is when the feminine strength in every soul is nurtured by a personal relationship with God, that a major breakthrough will occur in world transformation.

Brahma[1] put women in front, which would not have been an easy thing to do. He was able to make women see themselves differently and to bring them to a level of dignity and self-respect. Brahma had to play a unique role in order to achieve this. First, he had to develop all his own feminine principles and that is why he is fondly called the 'mother'. Only then could he look at these women with a vision of equality, deep respect and love.

I see Brahma as someone who took the risk of giving up his entire life for a 'message' that he received. That risk was based on the deep recognition he had, that once I change something inside me, I am not just doing it for myself; I am doing it for the whole world. That connection, between the individual and the world, is something that he taught me. Brahma was a family man and a businessman. The message that he shares is for us to change our lifestyles and through

---

[1] Founder of the Brahma Kumaris World Spiritual University

our profound transformation, change the entire world. It is a message that has universal appeal, a message that can spread across all layers of our society and our world, in terms of culture and religion, and actually touch the soul of every human being.

The greatest risk that Brahma took was to nurture the growth of women as spiritual leaders. Just imagine taking these innocent women without academic degrees or positions of influence in society, and training them to have spiritual impact and then saying to them, "Go out there and serve the world!" Brahma told them, "Don't have a crisis of loyalty, because your loyalty is to God alone." Today that loyalty is reflected in each of their lives in ways that no-one can challenge.

FRIENDSHIP

"When a friend needs help, I am able to give it very quickly. Soon afterwards, I forget that I have helped. I also do not want people to remember what I have done for them, because that creates a burden. To give, without having the desire to get something in return, is the purest friendship possible."

Chen
Businesswoman
China

IN THE BEGINNING, I just could not believe that raja yoga would change me. I worked in the US at the time and went to the meditation centre for quite a long period.

I thought that the face of my teacher was like a goddess, but I couldn't identify myself with her. I found the people at the meditation centre special and dedicated to the spiritual work, but saw myself as very ordinary. I didn't think that I would ever be able to change my life.

I went back to China, without realising that I had changed a lot. I used to worry about the future, lose my temper easily and shout at people at my work. But now it was very easy to manage my office without doing that. I wasn't speaking so fast any more and my voice was much more relaxed. Also my stress related health problems disappeared.

Still, I didn't want to be part of the organisation.

I went to the Brahma Kumaris headquarters in India, but said to myself that it would be the last time. I remember sitting on a swing, listening to some quiet music from my Walkman. I was crying and had such a heavy heart that I decided to leave the next day. The people were very good, but I just couldn't fully believe their knowledge.

As Chinese do not believe in God and there is no God in Buddhism, it was difficult for me to have this yoga link with God, especially the whole idea of Shiva, the incorporeal God.

How could I accept God to be an invisible point of light? Oriental people only believe something after they have seen or experienced it. Seeing and touching is believing.

In Buddhism, you learn from human beings like monks or famous people like Lao Tse and they are the ones you follow. In raja yoga, you don't find anyone like that in front of you. I could believe in Brahma, the founder, but they said that he wasn't God. I was confused and was longing for more clarity and insight.

Once I saw a Buddhist picture of someone who had a spiritual awakening. His forehead opened wide and wisdom came out of it. For years I had wished that would happen to me too.

Then whilst sitting on that swing, all of a sudden my third eye opened.

I could clearly see my spiritual self and also the immense beauty of life and I knew that I belonged to God.

There was absolutely no heaviness in my head any more and the sorrow I had felt disappeared. With this spiritual intelligence, I was able to understand the difference between physical and non-physical. Both are real. With my third eye, I could also see the unseen. I could see a wave of energy coming towards me and I could feel these loving, spiritual vibrations reaching my happy heart.

I saw things completely differently, as though I was in another dimension. I saw the beauty of the flowers, as I had never seen them before. With or without my glasses, they were the same, so I knew that I wasn't dreaming. I understood the inner side of life and from that moment my spiritual life truly began.

My present lifestyle is very different from the way I used to live. Previously I had left home at ten o'clock at night to go to dinner parties and then to the disco. I thought that was a normal life. If you are successful, you must have a night life. When my yoga teacher told me that it would be better to go to bed at 10pm, I thought that was crazy, perhaps something for lazy people. But I did change my life completely and now go to bed by 11pm at the latest, in order to get up early for my meditation.

My relationship with my husband also changed a lot. In a spiritual life, you no longer live as husband and wife, but more like brother and sister. We still felt love for each other, but my husband found that he also needed to have a physical relationship. So once in a while, he would have a girlfriend. When it became more serious with another woman, we decided to say goodbye. He remarried and now lives close by and we still have a very good relationship.

For me, sex was never that important. I noticed that without a physical relationship a woman becomes stronger. I also felt that type of relationship to be a burden. One has to think about someone else all the time. Now, when a friend needs help, I am able to give it very quickly. Soon afterwards, I forget that I have helped. I also don't want people to remember what I have done for them, because that creates a burden. To give, without having the desire to get something in return, is the purest friendship possible. It's real freedom.

SILENCE

"I love to be by myself in silence. That's the time to simply feel who I need to be. In solitude, there is a great sense of clarity, strength and stability. As an instrument for the Divine, it's my desire not to attract attention to myself, but to draw attention to God. And God is quiet."

Jenna
Personal Development Trainer
USA/Jamaica

BEFORE I BECAME a regular spiritual student, I had a strong attraction to material wealth and had a lot of friends. For a young single woman, I lived a very comfortable lifestyle. My friends' parents were children of the great personalities of those days, like prime ministers, presidents, mayors and politicians, and I used to enjoy extra good treatment. The lifestyle looked great, although sometimes I had no money in my pocket.

All of that changed when I became spiritual. Now I live an extremely simple life and yet my mind feels so wealthy. I now know that it is a great illusion to think that I am 'so and so' or this or that. I feel, as a woman, that first I need to take back my self-respect. I had somehow lost the ability to rule myself and was too sensitive. I became emotional when somebody said something to insult me. I still do not have full strength in my spiritual life to secure my heart and my feelings and I allow a percentage of other people's negative thoughts to affect me. When this happens, instead of being negative towards the person who is sending the arrow, I tend to beat myself up. Nevertheless, I am now learning to love and respect myself a lot more. It is about 65 percent successful, and it is based on a future me that I see.

One of the greatest aspects of love for myself is accepting who and what I am. This allows me to appreciate my own company. Just enjoying myself, watching my thoughts and entertaining my mind with thoughts that are based on wisdom and truth. Sometimes laughing at my own little idiosyncrasies.

Silence plays an important role when it comes to checking what's happening inside you. If you really go into your thoughts, you will come to understand why you are feeling the way you feel. I used to laugh a lot. It was a type of exercise for me, but now I also love to be in silence. That's my build-up, my power and my private time with God. That's the time to simply feel who I need to be, and how best God's energy can be facilitated. In solitude, there is a great sense of clarity, strength and stability. From that point on, when you come through, when you start to express your life, it's just got to be right, because you are, internally, what you are expressing externally. My desire, as an instrument for the Divine, is not to attract attention to myself, but to draw attention to God. And God is quiet.

Although I had no religious upbringing, I chose this path for God, or should I say, "He chose me". This is a question I still am not able to answer. My father was a Hindu from India, my mother a Catholic of African-Jamaican descent. One moment I could hear my father chanting, *"Hare, hare Krishna"* and being happy with his life, and the next moment my mother chanting, *"Mea culpa, mea culpa"* and crying. I used to look at both of them and think, "There is something wrong with this. What kind of God gives happiness to one and sorrow to another?"

Through studying the knowledge of raja yoga, I came to know God as the Bestower of happiness. I also learned how to simply have a union with Him. My relationship with God has been my primary objective in sorting out the world that lives behind my eyes, in the soul. It has also provided me with what I find most rewarding and practical for the 21st century.

When I was twenty-five, I began to have experiences in my dreams. They were like visions: seeing things that seemed to be real, but when you put your hand out, they were not there. When I went to India, on my own, in 1994, I had a profound experience of God. I was in a vast room of people, several thousand, and there was a senior yogi sitting on the stage. She went into trance and, when her eyes opened, it was as if there was this divine, supreme presence sitting inside that body. When those eyes touched my eyes, I was no longer in the same place; something of my past had been erased. The feeling was as if God was looking through those eyes, not the yogi. There was a subtle, silent, profound presence behind those eyes, looking through them and saying, "Welcome home, child, it has been a long time. It's so good to see you." I had the feeling that everything was okay; as if it were an awakened memory.

I believe that many souls today are carrying a burden of illusions resulting from their past experiences, whether of this life or of past lives. As a result, we have closed ourselves in and project images that conceal parts of us that are still tender, vulnerable or even forgotten. I'm no different, except that I took steps to change that and find out who I really am. In using the simple practice of a unique, spiritual and ancient wisdom known as raja yoga, I have been able to find a method that calls me to remember my original identity and pure sense of worth. It calls me to establish a connection with the Supreme Soul, and also to experience relationships with Him that are complete. I firmly believe that the world has lost its happiness due to what I call ALGAE (anger, lust, greed, attachment and ego); feelings that are inside the soul. Who can journey so deep inside of my being and be pure enough to remove them? Only God, the Supreme.

I have had the great fortune of being in contact and relationship with the leaders of the Brahma Kumaris. They are called Dadis, elder sisters, who constantly live values every moment that you see them, work with them, play with them, laugh with them. When I encountered these women, it inspired me so much because I saw these Dadis constantly 'creating'. One day I asked them, "What are the things you think of the most in our current times?" And they replied, "God and time." That is what I really value too and what we need to do at present is to keep busy in creating an elevated future, so that our past no longer exists.

PEACE

"Spiritual love is without desire or attachment. The only thing you want is happiness and peace. You just let the other person be. In silence, you start to develop a subtle form of communication. You communicate in a soul-conscious way, as soul brothers."

Teresa
Psychologist
Netherlands/Portugal

MANY THINGS HAVE changed in my life since I started to study raja yoga, including my relationship with my husband. I was strongly educated by my mother to become a good wife and mother myself. According to the Portuguese tradition, a

woman develops a deep attachment to her husband in order
to serve him, totally giving up her own life. This attachment
was one of the biggest issues I had to transform in my
spiritual life. I had to learn to be independent, whilst being in
a dependent relationship. I discovered that the many fears I
had were all connected to this attachment. There was the fear
of loss, the fear of making mistakes, the fear of just being by
myself etc. Within a dependent relationship, you lose a certain
part of yourself and I am still regaining that part of me.

When you are dependent on someone, you always put the
other ahead of you. There is no equality. Your husband is the
face of your relationship and your own face is hidden behind
it. In this way, you lose your own values and beliefs and this
becomes an attack on your self-respect. I lost my
independence and other values like self-trust and dignity.

In the pattern of serving the other person, you do things because
you are supposed to do them, according to the principles you
believe in and have accepted. But inside, you feel something
else. You ask yourself, "What about me? Where do I stand?
Who am I? What do I want?" You feel completely lost.

After both my husband and I had chosen this spiritual path,
we discussed all these things together. On a spiritual path,

you both like to be free and independent and, although we talked about it very openly and in an easy manner, I still felt it was very difficult to overcome my attachment to him. It seemed in opposition to my belief system and education.

At first, I tried to understand attachment and then to practise being more detached, letting my husband be more himself and also allowing me to be more myself. At a certain point, you think that you are getting there, but then you find that you have to face a more subtle form of attachment, which you hadn't yet realised was there.

Suddenly my husband got very sick and it appeared to be a very aggressive form of cancer, which the doctors said was incurable. This was the biggest test for me in detachment; I had to let go of him completely.

When I look back now, I can say that the period in which he was sick was the worst of my life. For about seven months, I suffered from fear, emotional and physical pain, and uncertainty. But in some ways, it was also a beautiful period, because I experienced true love, free from attachment. These were moments of pure love, which I had never ever experienced in all those years we had been together. It was silent love. We didn't need any words; we just looked into each other's eyes and understood everything. Because of my spiritual understanding of the soul, I was able to be more intimate and close to him than ever before. There was a different kind of intimacy.

Medically, we tried everything to cure him, but ultimately we both knew that we had to go into silence and just let it be. For many hours, days and weeks, I sat next to his bed in silence. He decided to spend his last few weeks at home with me. We said to each other that we were going to live these moments. It was the most silent time of my life. We were alone, just the two of us, and we lived in our own world of silence for months.

I knew that he had to go inside himself and that I too had to withdraw within in order to let go of him. We knew that the final separation had to take place.

The help that I received during that last period came from the spiritual understanding of the soul. I knew that the soul never dies, but rather lives eternally, and that all relationships are eternal, although there are different people around you in different incarnations. We both knew that dying was just letting go of the physical body.

He became very introspective and silent, also due to his severe pain. He just lay there with his eyes closed. I had to accept the situation.

In that silence, I talked to God and in my meditations I would ask Him how He could face His child suffering so much. For me, the most frustrating thing was that I couldn't help him when he was in pain. Then I realised that God was able to face it all, because He only saw the soul. He knew that it wasn't the end of the story, but rather a new beginning.

I started to see God as his Mother, strong and knowledgeful, embracing the pain of His child in silence. That idea gave me strength to stay beside him, trusting that finally all pain would finish.

In a way, I also had to die myself; but it was more like dying alive. I had to let go of all my desires, especially my desire to get my husband back. I couldn't keep him with me; I had to let go of him. These desires were causing me pain and again it was spiritual power that enabled me to give him all the love he needed. I also had to help him to break free from me. I said to him, "I am okay, whenever you want to go, just go." Saying this was like breaking my own heart, but I knew I had to do it. I had to see him as an individual with his own life and respect that individuality. After I took the decision to let go of him, I started to experience unconditional love. In those moments, I no longer had the desire to keep him with me. Voluntarily, I chose to let him go, although I had no other choice.

Spiritual love is without desire or attachment. The only thing you want is happiness and peace. You are both satisfied and, therefore, experience freedom. You share so much with each other without wanting or taking anything. You just let the other person *be*. We looked into each other's eyes without the need to say anything or to touch each other - just looking and knowing everything. In silence, you start to develop a subtle form of communication. We communicated in a soul-conscious way, as soul brothers.

Finally, I reached the stage of being very close to him and yet still detached. It was then that he felt he was free to go. When he was about to leave, I called his name, but then realised that I had to keep quiet in order to let him go. Very peacefully, very slowly, he went away without opening his eyes again. It was such a deep experience; painful, but beautiful, my last examination.

Without spirituality, it would have been hell. Even with spiritual power it had been difficult, but only because of my own belief systems and pain. The pain of attachment is very heavy when it comes to the point where you are forced to let go of someone you love.

His funeral was special and powerful, but when everything was over, I experienced an identity crisis. My whole identity, connected to my role, had finished. The only thing that I had left was myself.

I took his ashes to India, the country that was most important to him. I left him behind in the lake, near the place where he used to sit and meditate. It was a wonderful evening with a beautiful sunset. To take his ashes far away to his spiritual homeland and not keep them with me at home was my last lesson in detachment.

THE EDITOR

JACQUELINE BERG is a writer and teacher of raja yoga meditation living in Amsterdam, the Netherlands. Her professional background is journalism, which includes having been chief-editor for a magazine about health, spirituality and the environment. To bridge the gap between mainstream medical science and alternative ways of treatment, she initiated the Working Group for Spiritual Health, which has been organising symposia for many years for medical professionals. To encourage colleagues to investigate more deeply their personal responsibility as journalists and to stress the importance of ethical and spiritual media communication, Jacqueline has toured several countries to participate in media conferences. She is the designer of the **Positive Thinking** course, which is now being used all over the world. She has taught the art of Positive Thinking to different groups such as the police and medical personnel of several hospitals. As an optional part of a judicial rehabilitation programme in a prison in Amsterdam, the course helps drug addicts to achieve self-realisation and develop self-esteem. She has published two Dutch books, 'Geluk? Daar kom ik mijn bed niet voor uit! (**'Happiness? How boring!'**), followed by 'Engelengeduld' (**'The patience of a saint'**).

Other books to feed the soul

If you have enjoyed reading this book on Raja Yoga meditation as taught by the Brahma Kumaris World Spiritual University, you might like to read the following books to enhance your meditation practice and deepen your spiritual understanding.

Companion of God	Dadi Janki
God's Healing Power	BK Jayanti
Discover Inner Peace	Mike George
Eastern Thought for the Western Mind	Anthony Strano
Healing Heart and Soul	Roger Cole
In the Light of Meditation	Mike George
Inside Out	Dadi Janki
Pathways to Higher Consciousness	Ken O'Donnell
Practical Meditation	BK Jayanti
Restoring our Greatness	Dadi Janki
Soul Power	Nikki dé Carteret
The Alpha Point	Anthony Strano

All the above books and a variety of meditation commentaries and meditation music are available from
www.bkpublications.com

About the Brahma Kumaris World Spiritual University

The Brahma Kumaris World Spiritual University is an international organisation working at all levels of society for positive change. Established in 1937, the University now has over 8,000 centres in more than 90 countries. It actively participates in a wide range of educational programmes in areas such as youth, women, men, environment, peace, values, social development, education, health and human rights.

In 1996, the University's Academy for a Better World was opened in Mount Abu, India. The Academy offers individuals from all walks of life opportunities for life-long innovative learning. Residential programmes are centred on human, moral and spiritual values and principles. The University also supports the Global Hospital and Research Centre in Mount. Abu , India.

Local centres around the world provide courses and lectures in meditation and positive values, supporting individuals in recognising their own inherent qualities and abilities, and making the most of their lives.

All courses and activities are offered free of charge.

International Headquarters
Po Box No 2, Mount Abu 307501,
Rajasthan, India.
Tel: (+91) 2974-38261 to 68
Fax: (+91) 2974-38952
E-mail: abu@bkindia.com

International Co-Ordinating Office &
Regional Office For Europe And The Middle East
Global Co-operation House,
65-69 Pound Lane, London, NW10 2HH, UK
Tel: (+44) 208 727 3350
Fax: (+44) 208 727 3351
E-mail: london@bkwsu.com

REGIONAL OFFICES

Africa
Global Museum for a Better World,
Maua Close, off Parklands Road, Westlands,
PO Box 123, Sarit Centre, Nairobi, Kenya
Tel: (+254) 20-374 3572
Fax: (+254) 20-374 3885
E-mail: bkwsugm@holidaybazaar.com

Australia And South East Asia
78 Alt Street, Ashfield, Sydney, NSW 2131, Australia
Tel: (+61) 2 9716 7066
Fax: (+61) 2 9716 7795
E-mail: indra@brahmakumaris.com.au

The Americas And The Caribbean
Global Harmony House, 46 S. Middle Neck Road,
Great Neck, NY 11021, USA
Tel: (+1) 516 773 0971
Fax: (+1) 516 773 0976
E-mail: newyork@bkwsu.com

Russia, Cis And The Baltic Countries
2 Gospitalnaya Ploschad, Build. 1
Moscow - 111020, Russia
Tel: (+7) 095 263 02 47
Fax: (+7) 095 261 32 24
E-mail: bkwsu@mail.ru

http://www.bkwsu.org

Brahma Kumaris Publications
www.bkpublications.com
enquiries@bkpublications.com